D1017345

Rocket Science

By Deborah Lock

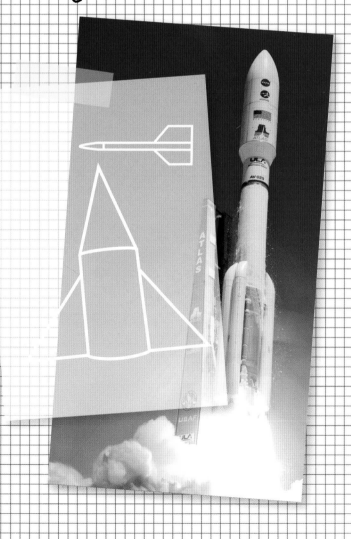

Series Editor Deborah Lock
US Senior Editor Shannon Beatty
Editor Nandini Gupta
Senior Art Editor Ann Cannings
Art Editor Dheeraj Arora
DTP Designer Anita Yadav
Picture Researcher Sakshi Saluja
Producer, Pre-production Ben Marcus
Managing Editor Soma B. Chowdhury
Managing Art Editor Ahlawat Gunjan
Art Director Martin Wilson

Reading Consultant Linda Gambrell, PhD

First American Edition, 2015
Published in the United States by DK Publishing
345 Hudson Street, New York, New York 10014

A catalog record for this book is available
from the Library of Congress.
ISBN: 978-1-4654-3581-1 (Paperback)
ISBN: 978-1-4654-3580-4 (Hardcover)

DK books are available at special discounts when purchased in bulk for sales promotions,
premiums, fund-raising, or educational use. For details, contact: DK Publishing Special Markets
345 Hudson Street, New York, New York 10014
SpecialSales@dk.com
Printed and bound in China.

A WORLD OF IDEAS:
SEE ALL THERE IS TO KNOW

Contents

Welcome to the laboratory! You must be the new lab assistant. Here you'll become a specialist in weird and wonderful natural science, forces in physics, explosive chemistry, and metal-changing alchemy. You might even become a crazy inventor after this! Now, you've just received a top-secret government assignment, and I hope you're ready for it. Are you ready to get to work?

Yes? Good! Then get ready for the assignment.

FOR YOUR EYES ONLY

Assignment: design a rocket for a spying mission

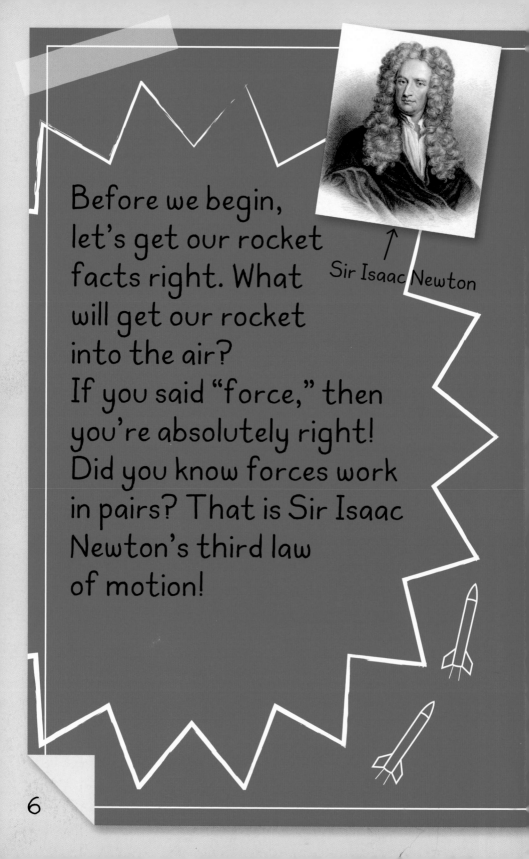

Before we begin, let's get our rocket facts right. What will get our rocket into the air?
If you said "force," then you're absolutely right! Did you know forces work in pairs? That is Sir Isaac Newton's third law of motion!

Sir Isaac Newton

LIFT
This force keeps the rocket stable in the air and controls the direction of the flight.

WEIGHT
The weight of a rocket is the force that pulls the rocket down.

DRAG
This force acts in the opposite direction to the thrust. It's caused by air getting in the way.

THRUST
This force needs power to lift the rocket off the ground, overcoming the weight and driving it forward.

Laws of Motion

In 1666, Sir Isaac Newton observed an apple fall from a tree. From that moment, he became very interested in invisible forces. During his further investigations, he discovered three simple laws that describe how forces make things move.

LAW OF MOTION 1

An object that isn't being pushed or pulled by a force either stays still or keeps moving in a straight line at a constant speed.

LAW OF MOTION 2

Forces make things accelerate. The bigger the force and the lighter the object ▷ the greater the acceleration.

LAW OF MOTION 3
Every action has an equal
and opposite reaction.

Sir Isaac Newton published these and other
math principles, in his book *Philosophiæ
Naturalis Principia Mathematica*
in July 1687.

Chapter 1
Materials

Let's get started!
First we need to decide
on what's best to use.
We need materials for
the following parts:

1. nose cone
2. fuselage
3. fins

There's got to be some bits and pieces that will be ideal somewhere around here. Come and take a look.

Remember, we need light things so our rocket can get moving faster, but the materials need to be strong, too.

Let's test what we have found.

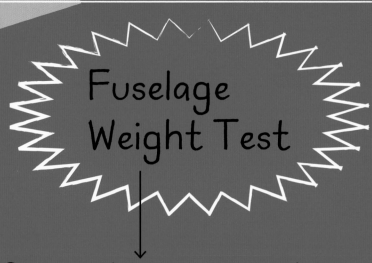

Fuselage Weight Test

1. Set up the spring weight test.

We will need:

pole

spring

hook

string

bucket

2. Place each item in the bucket.

one at a time

3. Measure the stretch of the spring, using a tape measure.

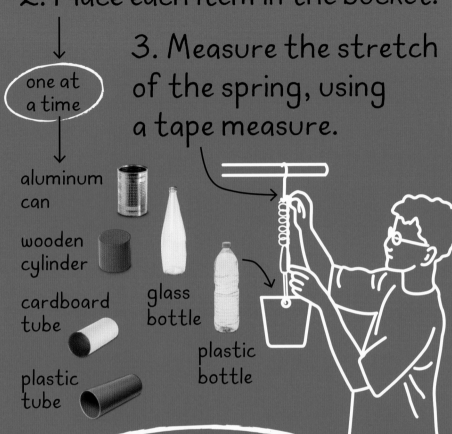

- aluminum can
- wooden cylinder
- cardboard tube
- glass bottle
- plastic bottle
- plastic tube

HOW SPRINGS WORK
Springs change shape when they are pulled by a force. The greater the pull, the greater they stretch. Many weighing machines use springs.

Nose Cone Weight Test

1. Set up the balance to compare the weight of each object.

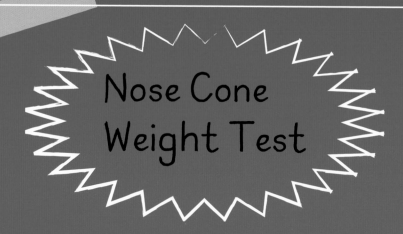

4 in.
(10 cm)

We will need:

plastic cup

Styrofoam cup

wooden toy cone

plastic cone

paper cone

cardboard cone

string tied around drawing pin in center of pole

adhesive putty
at either end

2. Attach two cone shapes, one on each end.

3. Each time, leave the lightest one on and add another to the other end.

HOW BALANCES WORK

Balances have a bar (lever) that tilts on a pivot (fulcrum). The loads are added on either side at the same distance from the fulcrum. If each load is equal, then the lever balances.

Fins Strength Test

We will need:

books

tablespoons of sand

plastic cup on string

bowl

materials

oak tag

paper

sponge

plastic

balsa wood

1. One at a time, lay each material across the gap and tape down the edges.

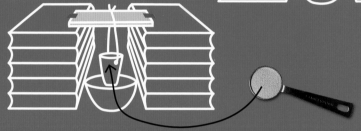

2. Pour tablespoons of sand into the cup until the material breaks.

3. Record the number of tablespoons needed.

Great work! We've tried and tested the materials to find the light but strong ones to use.

Rocket History

100BCE

Hero of Alexandria, an ancient Greek, invented an aeolipile. This was a rotating, sphere-shaped, rocketlike device powered by steam.

1200s-1400s

During this time, people experimented to improve solid-propellant rockets. For example, Jean Froissart in France discovered that launching rockets through tubes gave more accurate flights.

| 100BCE | 1CE | 1200 | 1400 |

1-1000CE

The Chinese invented fireworks for religious festivals. They filled bamboo tubes with gunpowder (a solid mixture). They then discovered that they could attach these to arrows, and that these could launch themselves.

1600s

The three laws of motion proposed by Isaac Newton, an English scientist, explained how rockets worked and have influenced rocket designs ever since.

1903

Konstantin Tsiolkovsky, a Russian schoolteacher, suggested the idea of space exploration by rocket, using liquid propellants.

1600   **1900**

1926

Robert H. Goddard, an American scientist, made the first successful flight of a rocket fueled by liquid oxygen and gasoline on March 16. It rose 40 ft (12.5 m) and landed 180 ft (56 m) away on a cabbage patch. A whole new stage in the history of rocket flight had begun!

Chapter 2
Design

Let's get to the drawing board. Which shape will work best? We want the air around the rocket to flow with minimum drag. The ideal shape can also help give better lift and less wobble.

We'll start with the fuselage shape. The tall, thin bottles should be faster and go farther. Let's do a throw test to see if that hypothesis is true!

1. Set up a test-throw area. Make sure no one is near you.

2. Stand on the same starting mark for each throw.

3. Throw the bottles— one at a time—with the same strength.

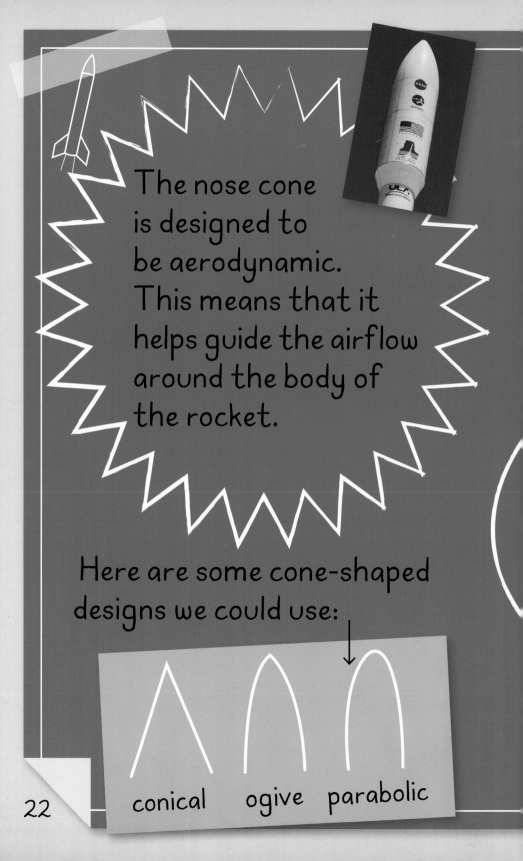

The nose cone is designed to be aerodynamic. This means that it helps guide the airflow around the body of the rocket.

Here are some cone-shaped designs we could use:

conical   ogive   parabolic

The shape of the fins can also affect the aerodynamics of the rocket.

basic fin designs

To decide which shape would be best for the rocket, let's attach the nose cones and fins to a bottle and test them in the lab's wind tunnel.

This wind tunnel will help us find out the best aerodynamic rocket.

1. SETTLING CHAMBER: this has screens and mesh to straighten the air.

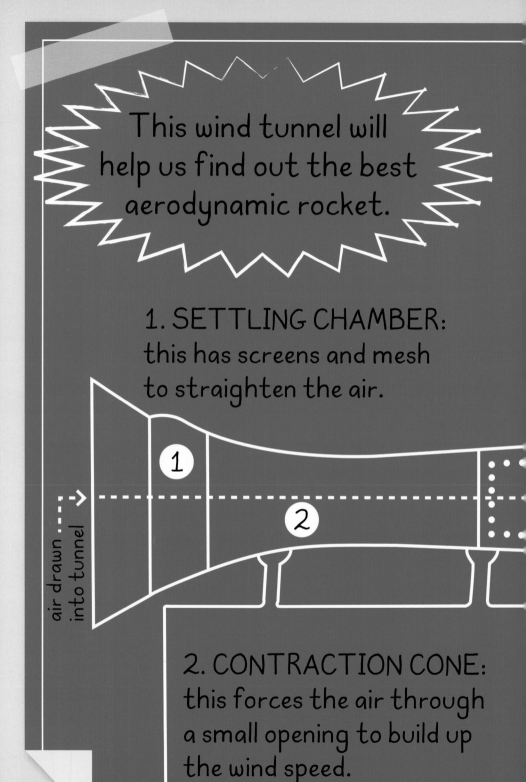

air drawn into tunnel

① ②

2. CONTRACTION CONE: this forces the air through a small opening to build up the wind speed.

3. TEST SECTION:
the model is mounted on sensors to record results.

4. DIFFUSER:
this keeps the air running smoothly to the end.

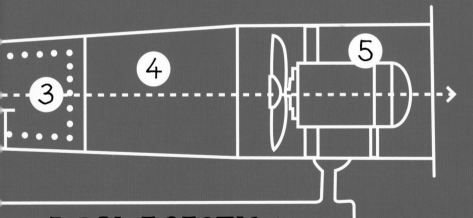

5. DRIVE SECTION:
the fan draws air into the tunnel by blowing it out. This gives the best control on the airflow.

The fins control the direction of a rocket's flight. They also keep the rocket stable when it's flying. Let's test to find the fins' best position.

Swing Test

1. Tie a long piece of string around a bottle with some fins attached. Move the string along until the bottle balances. This is the center of gravity.

2. Swing the bottle-rocket around your head.

CHECK: if the rocket points in the direction of the swing, then it'll be fine. If the rocket cartwheels, then the center of gravity and the center of pressure (where the wind pushes against it) are too close.

IMPROVEMENTS:
• add weight with some adhesive putty onto the nose cone...→
... or make the rocket longer to move forward the center of gravity.

• make the fins bigger and position them farther back to move back the center of pressure. →

Rocket Gallery

Rockets of all shapes and sizes have been developed and flown in the 20th century.

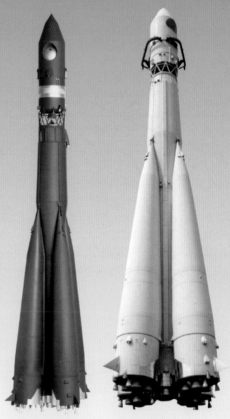

V-2 rocket, Germany: ballistic missile, first used 1944 during World War II

Redstone rocket, USA: surface-to-surface missile, launched August 1953

Sputnik 1, Russia: rocket with first satellite in space, launched October 4, 1957

Vostok, Russia: rocket carrying first human into space, launched April 12, 1961

Saturn V, USA: rocket with recoverable manned space capsule, first launched November 9, 1967

Titan III-Centaur, USA: rocket carrying probes to explore planets, first launched December 10, 1974

Space Shuttle, USA: reusable crewed spacecraft, first launched April 12, 1981

Our next challenge is to get the rocket into the air. We need an action that will cause a reaction to propel our pocket rocket.

This will show you why.

Stand on this skateboard.

Have a friend stand on this other one.

If you push each other, you will both move in opposite directions.

Space rockets zoom upward by the thrust of hot gases pushing downward.

fuel tanks

LIQUID-FUEL ROCKET ❯
The flow of the two fuels into the mixing chamber can be controlled for different bursts of power.

mixing chamber

igniter

solid fuel

❮ SOLID-FUEL ROCKET
Solid fuel burns with great power, but once started it can't be stopped.

Safety goggles on, please.
Let's test some ideas.

Fizzy Pressure Test

You will need:
a fizzy Vitamin C or
Alka-Seltzer tablet

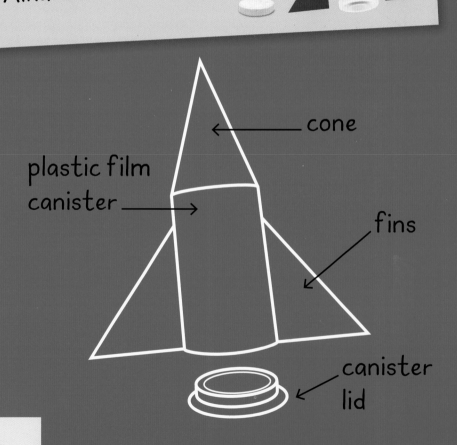

cone

plastic film
canister

fins

canister
lid

1. Put the tablet in the film canister, add a bit of water, and put on the lid.

2. Put the rocket down with the lid on the base, quickly.

3. Step away at least 7 ft (2 m) quickly. Watch it go!

(If it doesn't lift off, wait at least 30 seconds before checking.)

WHAT IS HAPPENING?
The water makes the tablet fizz. This fizz is a chemical reaction, which releases carbon dioxide gas. The gas builds up until it blows the lid off. This downward pressure makes the canister lift off.

33

Air Pressure Test

You will need:
a large plastic cup with no base,
two long balloons and tape

1. Blow up a balloon.
Pull the open end
through the cup.
Tape the end
to the outside.

2. Blow up the other balloon.
Push through the cup. This
keeps the first balloon closed.
Hold the end. Undo the tape.

3. Go outside for launch.

Stage 1

Let go of the second balloon.

Stage one is jettisoned.

Stage 2

WHAT IS HAPPENING?

When the rocket is released, the air rushes out of the end of the second balloon. The rocket is forced forward. As the air leaves, this balloon deflates. The balloon can't squash the neck of the other balloon any longer. So the air in the other balloon rushes out. The two stages help the rocket go farther.

Water Pressure Test

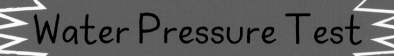

You will need:
bottle-rocket half-filled with water, cork, needle adaptor, and foot pump

1. Go outside and stand the bottle upside down on its fins.

2. Place the pump as far from the bottle as you can.

needle adaptor through cork

3. Start pumping.

(Don't approach the rocket because it will suddenly lift off.)

WHAT IS HAPPENING?

As air is pumped into the bottle, the air builds up inside. This air pushes harder and harder on the water. The force becomes so strong that it pushes the cork out of the bottle. The water rushes out downward and the bottle is pushed upward.

How Do Fireworks Work?

Once lit, the fuse (1) ignites the fuel propellant (2), sending the firework into the sky. Then the explosive magic happens!

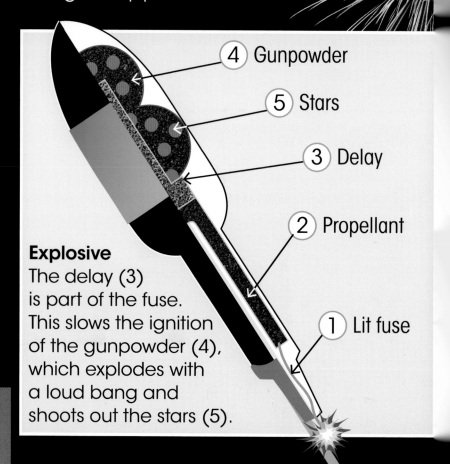

4 Gunpowder

5 Stars

3 Delay

2 Propellant

1 Lit fuse

Explosive
The delay (3) is part of the fuse. This slows the ignition of the gunpowder (4), which explodes with a loud bang and shoots out the stars (5).

BANG!

Colors in fireworks are created with
different chemicals. These are packed
into pea-sized nuggets called stars (5).
The chemicals glow when they get super hot.

Strontium creates red.

Barium creates green.

Sodium creates yellow.

Aluminum and magnesium
create blinding white light.

Chapter 4

Construction

The testing stage is complete. Let's use the results to construct our rocket.

First, attach three cardboard tubes together to make the rocket long and thin.

Push them inside each other to make them small to carry.

Fuselage: 3 cardboard
tubes of different
thicknesses

Nose cone: 1 plastic cone ⟶

Fins: cut from
4 oak tag ⟶

Engine: thin bottle half-
filled with water, fitted
with sports cap ⟶
Small bicycle pump with tube and
nozzle ⟶

1. Tape the tubes together
in order of size.
2. Tape the fins to the outside
of the largest tube.
3. Place the bottle inside
the largest tube, upside down.

Now it's time for the finishing touches.

This rocket will be used for a spy mission. We need to fix a tiny camera and bring the rocket safely back to the ground.

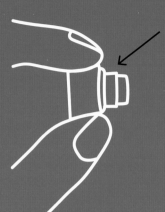

We can use this tiny spy camera.

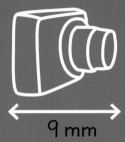

9 mm

It's only 9 mm long and it weighs 1 gram. It's state-of-the-art technology!

The light camera will not slow down the rocket.

Make a tiny hole through the top tube. Make the hole just large enough for the lens to poke out.

We need a rocket recovery system—something to slow down the descent of the rocket. A parachute or streamers could do the trick! Let's test some ideas.

You will need:

streamers made from strips of crepe paper →

← paper parachute with loop of thread attached at each corner

cloth parachute → with thread attached at four points

Descent Test

1. Attach each recovery system in turn to the same weight.
2. Raise your arm and release.
3. Count the number of seconds the weight takes to descend.

HOW PARACHUTES WORK

The large area of the parachute meets the large amount of moving air. This causes a large force of friction. At first, this is greater than the force of gravity pulling the weight down. The weight is slowed down to a steady speed for a safe landing.

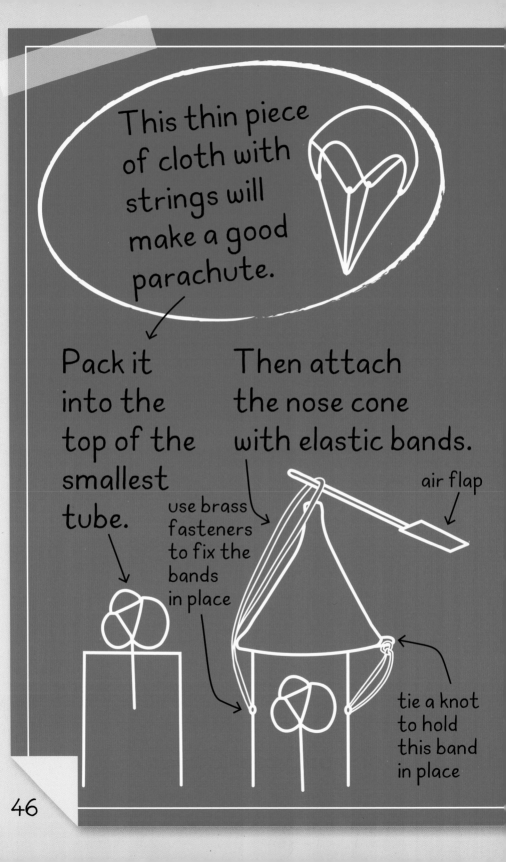

This thin piece of cloth with strings will make a good parachute.

Pack it into the top of the smallest tube.

Then attach the nose cone with elastic bands.

air flap

use brass fasteners to fix the bands in place

tie a knot to hold this band in place

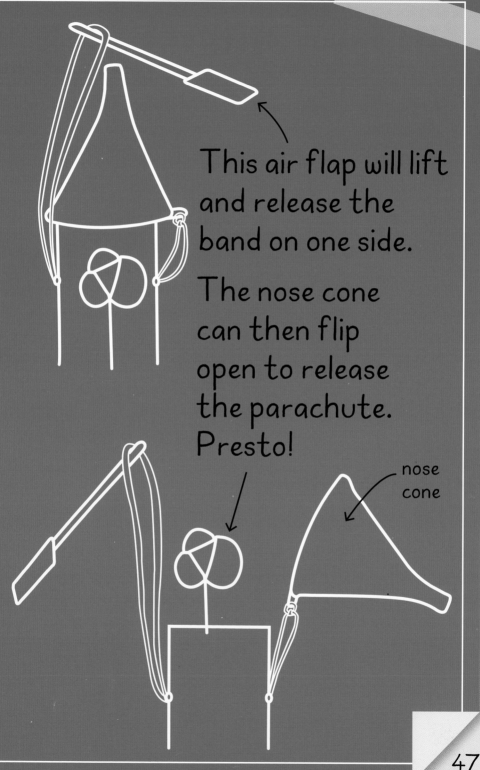

This air flap will lift and release the band on one side.

The nose cone can then flip open to release the parachute. Presto!

nose cone

Space Probes

Rockets have made it possible for scientists to send unmanned spacecraft packed with scientific instruments way out into space. These are called probes, which can send back information. There are three types of space probes: **interplanetary, orbiters,** and **landers**.

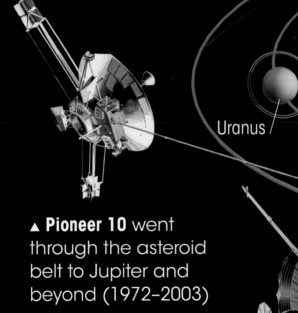

Jupiter

Uranus

▲ **Pioneer 10** went through the asteroid belt to Jupiter and beyond (1972–2003)

Galileo orbited ▶ Jupiter and its moons (1989–2003)

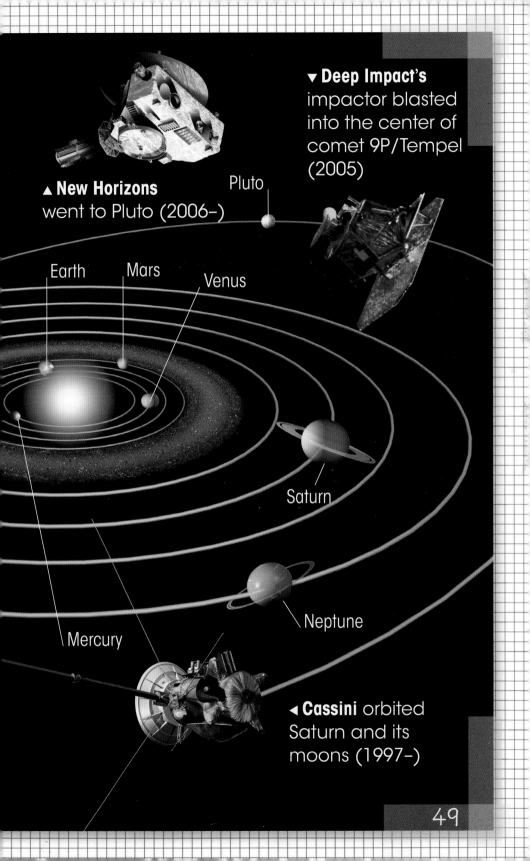

New Horizons went to Pluto (2006–)

Deep Impact's impactor blasted into the center of comet 9P/Tempel (2005)

Pluto

Earth   Mars   Venus

Saturn

Mercury

Neptune

Cassini orbited Saturn and its moons (1997–)

49

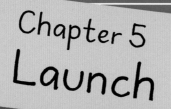

Chapter 5
Launch

Great work!
Our rocket is complete
and ready for launch.

Let's check
to see if it
passes the
safety rules.

upside-down
flowerpots for
launch stand

- ✓ Use lightweight, non-metal parts for body, nose, and fins.
- ✓ Launch outdoors, in open areas, and in good weather conditions.
- ✓ Launch at a 90 degree angle so the rocket will go straight up.
- ✓ Do not launch with people nearby.
- ✓ Do not launch at targets, into clouds, or near airplanes.
- ✓ Use a countdown before firing the rocket.
- ✓ If a rocket misfires, do not go near to disconnect the rocket for at least 60 seconds.
- ✓ Do not attempt to retrieve any rockets from tall trees, power lines, or other dangerous places.

Let's go for launch.

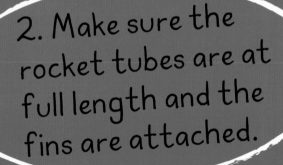

1. Switch the camera on and re-attach the nose cone.

2. Make sure the rocket tubes are at full length and the fins are attached.

3. Fill half the bottle with water, and then insert into the base tube.

4. Pull the bottle cap open and firmly push the pump nozzle into it.

5. Unravel the wire tubing and step back as far as possible.

5, 4, 3, 2, 1...
start pumping!

All systems are go.

Look! The air inside the bottle should be pushing against the water.

whoosh!
We have liftoff!

The water should force the nozzle right out of the lid and the jet should be gushing out. The rocket will then be powered upward. As the water leaves, the pressurized air inside the bottle will fill the space. This will also lighten the rocket's weight. Then as the pressure on the air lessens, the water jet will lessen, so the rocket's thrust lessens. The air pressure inside the bottle and the air pressure around the rocket will equalize.

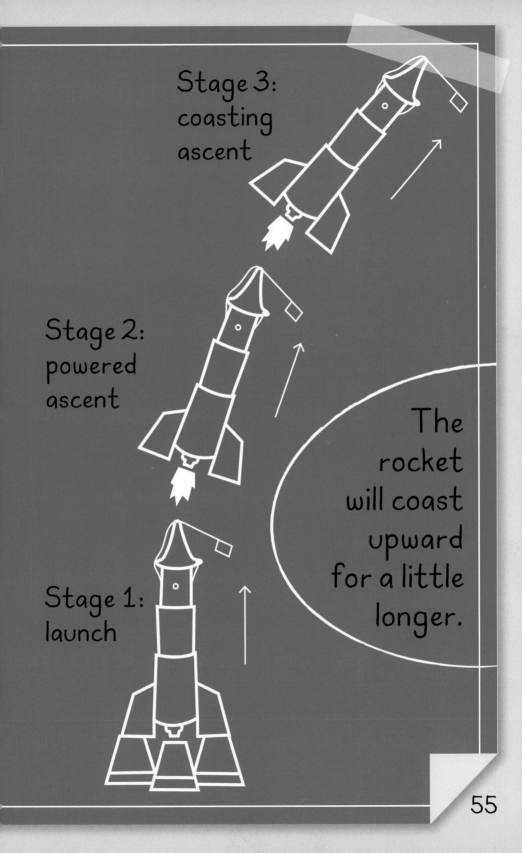

Stage 3: coasting ascent

Stage 2: powered ascent

Stage 1: launch

The rocket will coast upward for a little longer.

Now the weight and the drag of the rocket should slow it down. Maximum height has been reached.

The camera should be taking photos of a good view from up there. Now the rocket is falling down due to gravity. The air flap has released the nose cone. Look! The parachute is out. The rocket is slowing down to a safe speed for landing. It has landed and it's still intact. The camera is working fine, too. Success!

Mission accomplished!

Stage 4: maximum altitude

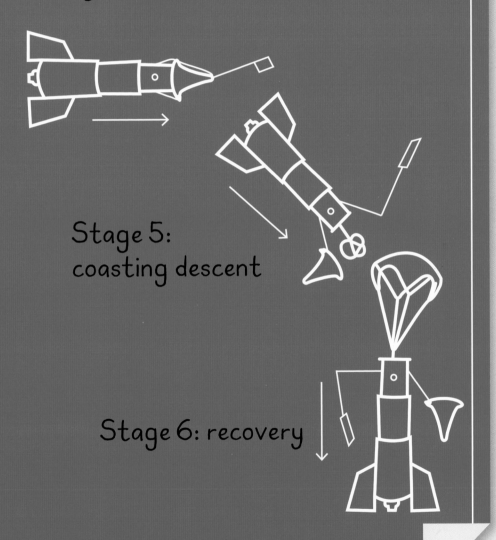

Stage 5: coasting descent

Stage 6: recovery

☞Introducing the All-new Spy Rocket!

Set it up and watch it blast off!

This **simple** but **effective** rocket is for any **spy** on assignment!

Perfect for a young cyclist on an **undercover mission**:

bag with rocket body inside

water bottle →

bicycle pump

- **compact** for carrying around
- **easy** to assemble
- **easy** to launch
- **easy** to recover
- **captures** aerial views of target on hi-tech camera

Rocket Science Quiz

1. What is Sir Isaac Newton's third law of motion?

2. What did the Chinese put inside bamboo tubes for fireworks?

3. Which Russian rocket carried the first human into space?

4. Which chemical makes yellow fireworks?

5. What did you use to power your spy rocket?

Answers on page 61.

Glossary

accelerate
move more
quickly

aerodynamic
able to help air
flow around
an object with
little drag

assignment
task or piece
of work

force
strength of an
action or movement

fuselage
main body of an
aircraft or rocket

ignite
light or catch fire

investigation
step-by-step test
or search to find
out facts

pressure
pushing force
on something

probe
unmanned
spacecraft

propellant
substance that
pushes a rocket
forward. The fuel
can be a solid
such as gunpowder,
or a liquid such as
liquid oxygen.

stable
steady object that
won't overturn

Index

Answers to the Rocket Science Quiz:
1. Every action has an equal and opposite reaction; **2.** Gunpowder; **3.** Vostok; **4.** Sodium; **5.** Water pressure.

Guide for Parents

DK Readers is a four-level interactive reading adventure series for children, developing the habit of reading widely for both pleasure and information. These books have an exciting main narrative interspersed with a range of reading genres to suit your child's reading ability, as required by the Common Core State Standards. Each book is designed to develop your child's reading skills, fluency, grammar awareness, and comprehension in order to build confidence and engagement when reading.

Ready for a *Reading Alone* book

YOUR CHILD SHOULD

- be able to read most words without needing to stop and break them down into sound parts.
- read smoothly, in phrases and with expression. By this level, your child will be mostly reading silently.
- self-correct when some word or sentence doesn't sound right.

A VALUABLE AND SHARED READING EXPERIENCE

For some children, text reading, particularly nonfiction, requires much effort, but adult participation can make this both fun and easier. So here are a few tips on how to use this book with your child.

TIP 1 Check out the contents together before your child begins:
- invite your child to check the blurb, contents page, and layout of the book and comment on it.
- ask your child to make predictions about the story.
- talk about the information your child might want to find out.

TIP 2 Encourage fluent and flexible reading:
- support your child to read in fluent, expressive phrases, making full use of punctuation and thinking about the meaning.

- encourage your child to slow down and check information where appropriate.

TIP 3 Indicators that your child is reading for meaning:

- your child will be responding to the text if he/she is self-correcting and varying his/her voice.
- your child will want to talk about what he/she is reading or is eager to turn the page to find out what will happen next.

TIP 4 Share and discuss:

- encourage your child to recall specific details after each chapter.
- provide opportunities for your child to pick out interesting words and discuss what they mean.
- discuss how the author captures the reader's interest, or how effective the nonfiction layouts are.
- ask questions about the text. These help to develop comprehension skills and awareness of the language used.

A FEW ADDITIONAL TIPS

- Read to your child regularly to demonstrate fluency, phrasing, and expression; to find out or check information; and for sharing enjoyment.
- Encourage your child to reread favorite texts to increase reading confidence and fluency.
- Check that your child is reading a range of different types of material, such as poems, jokes, and following instructions.

Series consultant, **Dr. Linda Gambrell**, Distinguished Professor of Education at Clemson University, has served as President of the National Reading Conference, the College Reading Association, and the International Reading Association. She is also reading consultant for the **DK Adventures**.

Have you read these other great books from DK?

Meet the sharks who live on the reef or come passing through.

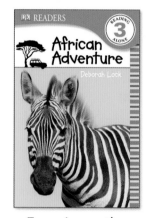

Experience the thrill of seeing wild animals on an African safari.

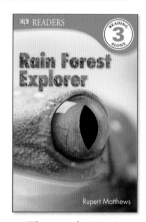

Through Zoe's blog, discover the mysteries of the Amazon.

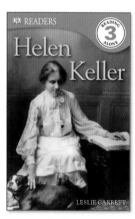

Read about the remarkable story of the deaf-blind girl who achieved great things.

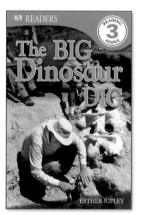

Josh and his team dig up dinosaur bones in a race against time.

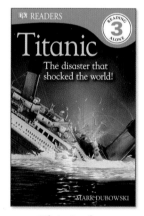

This is the incredible true story of the "unsinkable" ship that sank.